SHADES OF LIFE

RAHUL B R

Contents

About Publication

Words of Soul is a writing Community, where we have a group of new budding writers with their talent of framing emotions into words.

Formed by Dr. Nikita Dudagi and Lucky Pandey on May 15th 2021 to encourage and appreciate the enthusiastic writers. Weekly Special events and programs are being conducted to recognise the best Writer of the community. Words of Soul, a Group of Aspiring writers who ink the emotions of their heart to inspire the reader's mind.

Words of Soul Publications is not only a publication, it's a kind of family of writers which includes Co-author, writer, Author, compiler, co-compiler, Graphic Team, Project Heads, CEO, co-founder and Founder. Here Everyone is free to give their ideas and we initiate their actions.

Acknowledgements

The completion of this book would not have been possible without the help of my parents, friendsand also the publication "Words Of Soul". So thank them all whole heartedly for supporting and helping me in every step. So I am dedicating this book of mine to them...

About The Book

The book SHADES OF LIFE upholds the beauty of imagination and thoughtful process... more over it creates a good impression and impact on love, life, life journey, time and much more. It shows the imaginary part of each and everything. It will also grow the readers confidence level to the other level where they can get comfort in every thing and in every single situation on reading...

Author Of The Book

RAHUL B R

He is Rahul.B.R

He was born on 19/09/1999 Ramanagara district, Karnataka.

But he is perceiving his higher studies in Bangalore. He has completed bachelor degree in science. He like to know more about literature and want to study more and more about it…

He started writing poems from past four years and he writes all kinds of poems… on life, about nature's beauty, love and much more. He is coauthored in many books, Compiler of the book called "The Song Of Nature", "Nemophilist", "The Song Of Paradise", "Wings To Your Thoughts" and "The Unchosen Bond" and few more… He is also an author of a book called "GUIDE OF THOUGHTS By God's Grace",

and his poems has been published in his college magazine too.

1. LOVE

Love is blind
Keep it in mind,
There is no end
No future, past and demand.
Love is hard to find
Keep it in mind,
It can communicate end to end
Without any disturbing command.
Love can create an unimaginable bond
Keeping it safe it's in your hand,
Always be with it and understand
From the bottom of the soul and mind.

2. TIME

Everyone has 24 hours,
Some feel it's less,
And some with no response.
Time, it's very precious…
Other than the other things,
No-one can understand its…
Way of coming in presence.
Some value perfect timings,
Rather than unusual nonsense.
It may feel short on duties,
But feels long for lazy.
It's one among beautiful creations,
Where no-one recreate or performes.
With lots of multi characters,
It is present with us…

3. BE...

Burn like a sun
Roar like a lion
Shine like a star
Brave like a warrior
Sharp like a needle
Act like a double
Float like a cloud
Shift like a sand
Grow like a tree
Group like a bee
Attack like a tiger
Think like a terror
Handle like a common man
End like a gentleman .

4. BELIEVE

In today's world,
Many are not bold,
Hard to believe someone....
To believe there is no-one.
There may be some or the other,
But no near may be far...
Only some are truthful,
To believe in this whole.
Believe is like hope which attain,
To the stage particular main....
It's hard to describe or to define,
And also hard to believe with fine.

5. THE METAL

As strong as Osmium,
As weak as Tin...
As precious as Rhodium,
As poisonous as Mercury...
As rare as Lanthanum,
As tensile as Tungsten...
As reactive as Lithium,
As active as Rubidium...
As malleable as Gold,
As available as Aluminum...
As conductor as Silver,
As non conductor as Carbon...

6. THE UNTOUCHABLES

People think untouchables are impure,
And make them to come across, to suffer...
Not suppose to enter in the temple,
Not suppose to drink water from wells,
Not suppose to enter in the class room,
And not suppose to get proper education..
Everyone thinks about caste and religions,
But never thought we all are Indians...
Everyone on this mother earth,
Has equal rights to live and to take birth...
Untouchables are lakhs together,
But still none of them bother...
Still they are treated like slaves,
Not like the true Indian citizens...
Many people fought against it,
And still today they are fighting...

7. LIPS

There is nothing as soft as,
Your bright red lips…
It's as fresh as roses,
And tender as clouds.
My eyes search for your lips,
Even if you are far in miles…
Your beautiful smile,
Is always my profile…
I like to put my finger,
On your lips in winter,
To make them warmer
It's my only wish Dear…

8. YOUR EYES

The first day I saw your eyes,
I was really surprised,
It was like sunrise…
When ever I see your eye,
I feel really shy,
I truly don't know why…
Your cute little eyes,
Makes me to fly high,
In the light blue sky…
I am not saying lies,
Everyday I see your eyes,
To forget my stress…

9. Dr. B R AMBEDKAR

Grown in a poor family,
Builded his future very bravely,
In front of him everyone are equal,
He made everyone wish fulfill.
He din't discriminated anyone,
And never disappointed anyone,
Aim was to destroy the caste system,
And provide equal freedom.
The whole world will recognise him,
Saying the words "Jai bheem".
He conquered abundant knowledge,
And constructed many hermitage.
He opened everyone's eyes…
But, lived for very few years
Which was a great loss for us…

10. MY LIFE

What should I do, dear life...
Now you have become a dry leaf,
Whom should I believe,
And with whom should I live.
My brain is now blank,
And thoughts are stuck.
My life changes time to time,
To lead this life I feel shame,
Now I am burden on the earth I feel,
How can I know the good path...
Here, there is no value for honest peoples,
And no value for silence.
My life is becoming worst day by day,
And now I am tired by searching the new way.

11. WE ARE BEST FRIENDS (Part 1)

We are third bencher boys,
And we don't make noise,
We use local brands,
But, we are the Kings.
Break all the rules,
But never forget to respect others.
We are not cowards,
And we never lend,
Law is in our pockets,
Knowledge is in our hands.
Always seen in happy mood,
Never get tired or bored...
At any cost we never change place,
Because, we are the best friends...

12. WE ARE BEST FRIENDS (PART 2)

We all are brave,
Take part in every role.
Interested in all subjects,
No one dare to command us…
Everyone talk about our attitude,
Because, we maintain some standard.
We involve in others feeling,
And fulfill their problems and everything.
Our friendship is too strong,
It will always prolong,
Capable of doing everything,
Trying to invent more interesting.
We like to rule the world,
And we truly are very bold,
So everyone say "They Are Royal Gold"…

13. MOON

Moon is one of the natural satellite,
Which shines with the help of sun light,
It looks like a bright spot, in the black night.
Everyone wants to see it in their own sight,
There is not even a single person,
Who hate the moon.
On the day of full moon night,
It shines really very bright.
Looks more beautiful, when stars are beside,
So to learn about it, choose as a perfect guide.
If the beauty of moon is gone,
Then people will forget about heaven,
The moon may be too far from us,
But, it keeps smile on everyone faces.

14. THE BEGGARS

We see many beggars in our daily life,
Working tremendously day and night,
To make their future bright…
They are always calm and silent,
And very much innocent,
Badly suffering in pain,
Without having shelter to protect from rain.
People give ten or twenty to them,
Which they can't earn in their dream,
Due to loss of an organ.
Some will be in their own world,
Suffering with disease including cold.
Their life and future is full of miseries,
And living depends on begging.

15. BANGALORE CITY

City of all citizens,
Not just Indians…
People here work day and night,
To make their future bright.
They are here to fulfill their dream,
Without wasting any time,
Students come for studies,
And to build the careers,
People try for the success,
By their never ending attempts.
People in this city are smart,
And also show love towards art.
City of all citizens,
Not just Indians…
People here work day and night,
To make their future bright.
They are here to fulfill their dream,
Without wasting any time,
Students come for studies,
And to build the careers,
People try for the success,
By their never ending attempts.
People in this city are smart,
And also show love towards art.

16. COVID-19

The devil has arrived once again,
But please don't be afraid,
It may cause you disease,
But not the death of course.
Follow the rules and regulations,
Like social distancing
By using mask and sanitizer.
Have trust in yourself,
With lots of positive immunity,
Because, it's the true vaccine.
Please be aware of it,
Without neglecting it.
People, the last words to you
"Your health is in your hand"…

17. WE TOO HAVE HEART

Do you know what?
We too have heart…
Which can understand,
And connects end to end.
We too have emotions,
Which comes in every situations.
We too cry and laugh,
And like to be cared safe.
We too feel scared,
Somewhat weird…
Understand it,
But never doubt.

18. NEVER LEAVE ME ALONE

I always remember the time,
And days which we spent.
You came to my life
And changed it,
Picked me from the earth,
And kept me to the sky.
I will never get a friend like you,
I should say that I am blessed to have you,
The world will remember,
Our friendship story after our death too,
That's my promise and that's the truth.
I can't live without you,
I like to be with you.
And live with you now and for ever…

19. YOU...

I will regain what I have lost,
Because, you are my life
And the inspiration,
No-one can inspire me,
Except you my dear friend…
So come fast as possible.
I will be waiting for you,
In the same old place,
Where you left me before.
You are my everything,
Except you I have nothing,
So come and join me
Once again…
I will be waiting for you
Again and again…

20. REMEMBER

KNOWLEDGE AND EXPERIENCE,
WILL GIVE THE POWER TO SURVIVE.
A GOOD CHARACTER,
WILL PROVIDE THE RESPECT.
SO MAKE SURE…
YOU HAVE ALL THIS
IN TODAY'S LIFE.

9 798888 698020